Dedicated to all of the little globetrotters around the world.

PAYTON GOES TO
London

BY

SHAYLA MCGHEE AND PAYTON MCGHEE

Payton woke up and raced to the bathroom to brush her teeth and wash her face.

Today was an exciting day.

She and her family were traveling to London.

After she put on her clothes, she looked at the map on the wall to find the city of London.

Atlantic Ocean

SCOTLAND

North Sea

IREL...

ENGLAND

London

"There it is!" She pointed.
"London is the capital of the United Kingdom,
a country located on the continent of Europe."

"Ready?" Mom asked as she peeked through the door. "Ready!" Payton exclaimed.

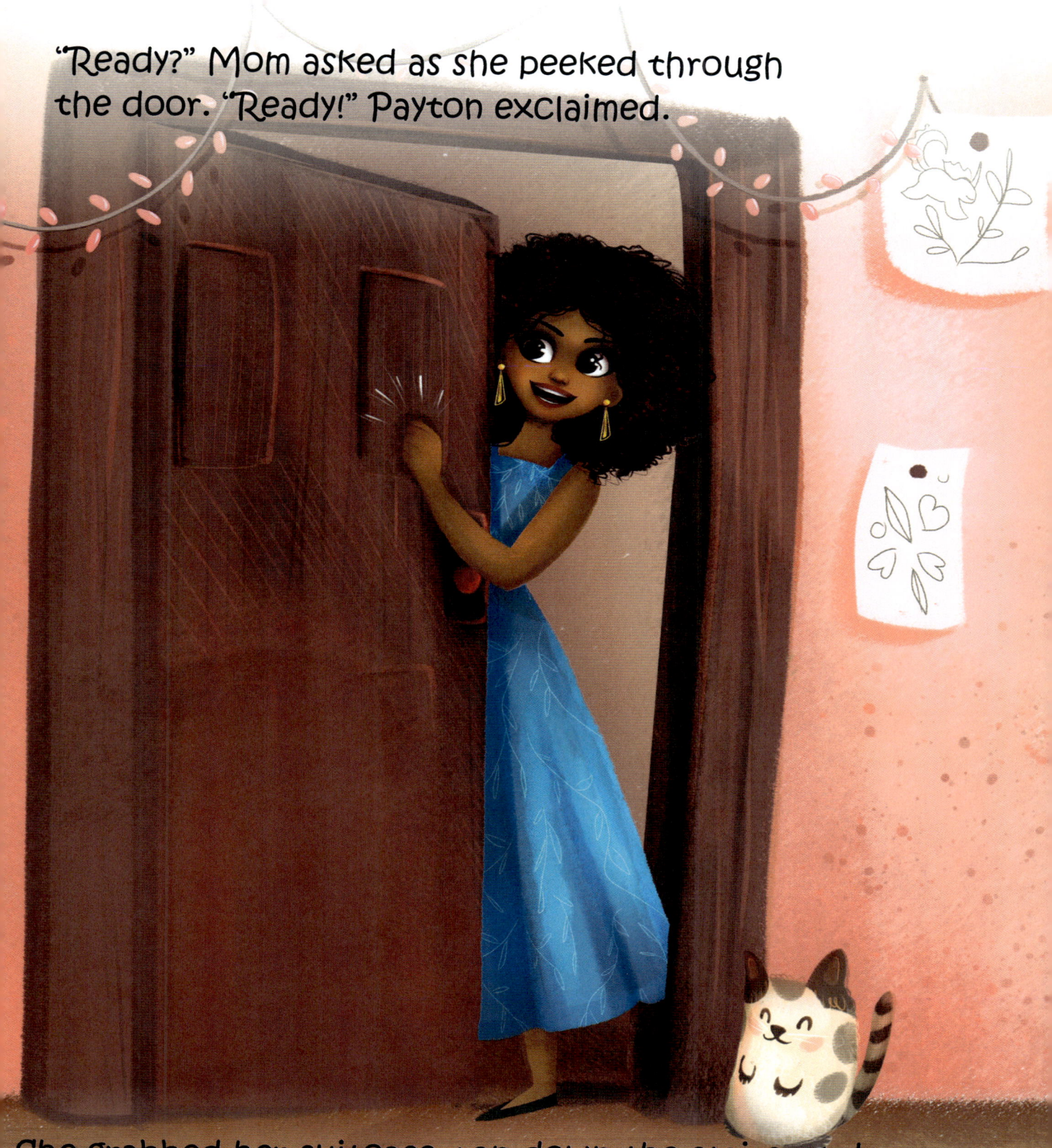

She grabbed her suitcase, ran down the stairs, and hopped in the car with her mom, dad, little brother, and little sister. The next stop was the airport.

The flight to London was long, but Payton was well prepared.

She brought coloring books as well as her favorite toys and talked with her family.

The airplane even had movies to watch and snacks to eat. After a long nap, they landed in London.

The first thing they did was take a train named the Heathrow Express to Paddington Station.

Her brother and sister loved the train ride. "Bye-bye, choo choo train," they yelled as it left the station.

Next, Mommy and Daddy took them to Hyde Park.

They enjoyed making wishes at the fountains and visiting the Rose Garden, but they loved going to the playground and making new friends most of all.

As they left the park, Payton saw a giant bus.

"Wow! I've never seen a bus like that before."

"It's called a double-decker bus," her dad explained.
"Let's all take a ride."

They hopped on the bus, and Payton went to the top to get a better view of London as it took them around the city.

From the top, she saw Big Ben. The tall tower's clock looked amazing and the bell inside rang as they passed by.

The bus stopped and let them off next to the London Eye. Payton had never seen a wheel so big, but she was excited to get on.

As they went higher and higher, her sister grabbed her legs.

"It's okay. Don't be afraid," Payton said, giving her sister a reassuring hug.

Next, they hopped on a boat that took them down the River Thames. They could see the Tower Bridge from the water.

Their last stop was Buckingham Palace.

Payton loved seeing the guards march back and forth in their red coats and tall, black, furry hats.

"I wonder what it would be like to have tea with the queen," she thought.

On their way to the hotel, they paused to eat at a beautiful restaurant decorated with pretty pink, yellow, and white flowers. They ordered fish and chips, which is a popular dish in London.

"In London, French fries are called chips," she explained to her brother.

As the day came to an end, Payton looked up at her parents and gave them great big hugs.

"Thank you for bringing us here," she said. "I can't wait for our next family adventure!"

ABOUT THE AUTHORS

Shayla McGhee

Born and raised in Georgia, Shayla McGhee graduated Summa Cum Laude from Spelman College where she received her Bachelor of Arts in Political Science with a minor in Secondary Education. After completing her undergraduate studies, Shayla attended the University of Georgia School of Law and is a current member of the Georgia Bar. Her expertise in education afforded her the opportunity to create digital content for the state of Georgia. In addition to writing, she enjoys traveling and spending time with her family and friends. Find out more about Shayla and her family on Instagram @shaylatmcghee and @mcgheepartyof5.

Payton McGhee

Payton McGhee has a love for rainbows, unicorns, and of course, travel. In just a few short years, she has had the opportunity to visit Belgium, France, Holland, and England. When she is not writing in her journal, she can be found spending time with her family, playing with her friends, and participating in extra-curricular activities such as gymnastics and track. For more from Payton, subscribe to her YouTube channel, Payton's Playful Adventures.

www.sableinspiredbooks.com   Facebook: @sableinspiredbooks   Instagram: @sableinspiredbooks

Made in the USA
Las Vegas, NV
25 July 2023